GW01110852

A STORY TO TELL

Also published by
University of Western Australia Press
for the Charles and Joy Staples
South West Region Publications Fund:

A Tribute to the Group Settlers
Philip E. M. Blond

For Their Own Good
Anna Haebich

Dearest Isabella
Prue Joske

Portraits of the South West
B. K. de Garis

A Guide to Sources for the History of South Western Australia
complied by Ronald Richards

Jardee: The Mill that Cheated Time
Doreen Owens

Blacklegs: The Scottish Colliery Strike of 1911
Bill Latter

Barefoot in the Creek
L. C. Burton

Ritulalist on a Tryicycle: Frederick Goldsmith Church, Nationalism and Society in Western Australia
Colin Holden

Western Austsralia As It Is Today, 1906
Leopoldo Zunini,
Royal Consul of Italy
edited and translated by
Richard Bosworth and Margot Melia

The South West from Dawn till Dusk
Rob Oliver

Contested Country
Patricia Crawford and Ian Crawford

Orchard and Mill: the Story of Bill Lee, South-West Pioneer
Lyn Adams

A Naturalist's Life
Rica Erickson

Richard Spencer: Napoleonic War Naval Hero and Australian Pioneer
Gwen Chessel

The Charles and Joy Staples South West Region Publications Fund was established in 1984 on the basis of a generous donation to The University of Western Australia by Charles and Joy Staples.

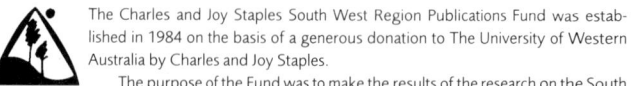

The purpose of the Fund was to make the results of the research on the South West region of Western Australia widely available so as to assist the people of the South West region and those in government and private organisations concerned with South West projects to appreciate the needs and possibilities of the region in the widest possible historical perspective.

The fund is administered by a committee whose aims are to make possible the publication (either by full or part funding), by University of Western Australia Press, of research in any discipline relevant to the South West region.

A STORY TO TELL LAUREL NANNUP

The Charles and Joy Staples
South West Region Publications Fund

University of Western Australia Press

First published in 2006 by
University of Western Australia Press
Crawley, Western Australia 6009
www.uwapress.uwa.edu.au
for The Charles and Joy Staples
South West Region Publications Fund

This book is copyright. Apart from any fair dealing for the purpose of private study, research, criticism or review, as permitted under the Copyright Act 1968, no part may be reproduced by any process without written permission. Enquiries should be made to the publisher.

Copyright © Laurel Nannup, 2006

The moral right of the author has been asserted.

National Library of Australia
Cataloguing-in-Publication entry:

Nannup, Laurel.
    A story to tell.

    ISBN 1 920694 70 6
    ISBN 978 1 920694 70 8

    1. Nannup, Laurel—Childhood and youth. 2. Women,
    Aboriginal Australian—Western Australia—Biography.
    3. Nyungar (Australian people)—Biography. 4. Aboriginal
    Australians—Western Australia—Social life and customs.
    I. Title.

994.10049915

Cover: Laurel Nanup: Lolly Tree, Woodcut 2001

Consultant editor: Venetia Somerset
Designed and typeset in Foundry Sans by Becky Chilcott, Chil3, Perth
Prepress by Hellcolour, Australia
Printed by Everbest Printing Co., China

DEDICATION

For my son Brett Nannup, and his daughter Lily Wilson.
For my son John Williams and his children.
For my son Charles Williams and his children.
And to my parents Renee and Peter Nannup, who have

CONTENTS

Acknowledgements ix

STORIES
Introduction 2
The Dream 6

FAMILY DAYS
My Gran 10
Big Mum, Little Mum 14
Dad and the Haystack 16
Hunting with Dad 18
Beansticks and Christmas 22
Cutting Fence Posts 24
Pinjarra Racetrack 26
Wagging School 30
First Holy Communion 32
Camp Fire 34
The Lolly Tree 36

MISSION DAYS
The Big Black Car 40
My First Christmas Card 42
Farm Work 44
Sliding Sister 48
Birthday Party 50
Pumphreys Bridge 52
Father Wellems' Garden 54
Springtime 56
Gum-picking 60
Girls Gone Walkabout 62
That Old Mission Bus 64
Goodbye Wandering 66
Mission Mates 68

ACKNOWLEDGEMENTS

For Vicki O'Shea, Marion Pearson and Harry Hummelsten, thank you for your advice and help at Curtin University. Also to Sandy Toussaint, John Stanton and Brett Nannup for the help you have given me. A big thank you to the staff at UWA Press.

STORIES

These stories are of my experiences as a young child and a teenager. I feel I need to leave some stories behind.

It is important for me to record my stories because throughout my younger life I felt I didn't know much about my culture, except the little bits Dad told me. My son would often ask me things about my culture and I felt I had no stories to tell. But once I started at Curtin Uni and got talking with other Nyoongars, I began to remember certain things that happened in my life and I realised that these are my stories. They are my life.

After looking through my old photographs, many memories stirred. I thought of when we lived in the bush, helping Dad and Mum work, and back to the days when we lived on the reserve in Pinjarra. Then there were the happy times with my grandparents, uncles, aunties, cousins, brothers, sisters, but most of all my nan, Tottie (Christine) Hart. I have lots of memories of the Wandering Mission, some sad and some happy ones. I would like to thank the Sisters who looked after us at the Mission. Thank you for caring for all the girls and boys. Thank you.

I saw an exhibition of art works by Salvatore Zofrea, where he told his life story through woodcuts. This gave me the idea

Untitled
Etching 2001

of telling my stories about my family and Mission life. To me his prints were the best and I was very inspired by his work.

My etchings and woodcuts are just another way to tell my stories; they are a way of communicating with people. I would like people to look at the smaller pictures as if they were looking through the eyes of a child. The three larger text pieces are more to do with me trying to remember my stories and trying to catch hold of my memories.

Untitled
Etching 2001

THE DREAM

Towards the end of last term, I felt that I could not go on at Curtin Uni. I just felt very tired. One night in my sleep I had a dream. It was so real. I was standing in the bush, with lots of trees around, and there were two dirt roads, one going to my left and one going to my right. As I stood there looking up those roads, to my left in the distance I could see an old Nyoongar man coming towards me until he got so close that he stood right in front of me. I looked at him, he looked at me, and then he said, 'What road are you going to take?'

I woke up with a fright, not because of the old man but because it seemed so real.

After the dream, I decided to continue on at uni. I believe he was my grandad telling me to finish my studies. I felt much happier about things then.

What road are you going to take?
Etching 2001

FAMILY DAYS

MY GRAN

This etching print is of my grandmother, Mrs Tottie Hart. She married Jack Hart and they had thirteen children, five boys and eight girls. Gran also had two lots of twins.

My gran was blind for as long as I can remember her, and had a cane so she could find her way around. Gran mainly lived down south, around the Darkan, Collie, Williams district. Years later she moved to Perth. Her son Lionel and daughter-in-law Ethel used to look after her as she could no longer look after herself.

One day when we lived on the Pinjarra reserve, Gran decided she was going to chop firewood, so off she went, a blind lady going to get wood. My sister Cecilia, a three-year-old, followed her. They never found the bush but ended up downtown in the main street of Pinjarra, Gran with an axe over her shoulder and my little sister in tow.

Years ago, when we lived at Darkan, Gran went to Collie to pick up her pension and to do some shopping. She asked me to go along to help her and she promised to buy me a new dress. We caught the bus into Collie. At the shop there I saw a pretty dress that I liked. It had red roses on it and it cost ten shillings. Gran got really cross at me for wanting that dress, but at the end of our argument she gave in and I got my dress with

Granny Hart
Etching 2001

the pretty red roses. When I think of it, I suppose for Gran that was a lot of money. In those days after our shopping we caught the bus back to Darkan. Gran was still grumpy, and we were happy to get back home.

Gran was a remarkable woman. In her young days she used to be a good horsewoman and could ride as well as a man—you see Gran told me this story many years ago. She was 96 years old when she passed away at Mt Henry Hospital. At the time she was there, so was one of her daughters. Gran is buried at the Collie cemetery in the same grave as her husband.

In the end I got my dress, with the pretty red roses
Etching 2001

BIG MUM, LITTLE MUM

Before Mum and Dad were married I lived with my Uncle Henry and Aunty Alma. Uncle Henry was a big man with a pot belly, and Aunty Alma was a skinny lady. They were just the opposite of each other in build. To me they were Big Mum and Little Mum.

So Uncle Henry became my mum and that's what I called him, Mummy. One day Uncle Henry was arrested for something or other, and Aunty and I went to see him in jail. Aunty told me I just cried for my Mummy. The policeman's wife couldn't understand why I was calling my uncle 'Mummy', so my aunty had to explain that was what I called my uncle. I don't know how long I stayed with my uncle and aunty, but I do know that I was the first of many foster children they looked after.

Aunty Alma and
Uncle Henry Dinah

DAD AND THE HAYSTACK

In the early days, there were only about five kids in our family. Dad worked for a dairy farmer just outside Pinjarra. One day I came home from school and found Dad laying down near the haystack. Being only young, I sat down next to him and started to cry—he just wouldn't wake up.

I walked to where our shack was, but Mum and the kids were not there. I felt so alone, I thought everyone had left me. So off I went back to Dad, who was still lying down, and I did some more crying. After a time Dad woke up, saw me there and said, 'why didn't you wake me'!

Afterwards it was about time for the cows to be milked so I helped Dad in the dairy. When work was all finished and we got our two bottles of milk we went back to our camp to get the old bike. Dad and I then went into Pinjarra to look for Mum and the kids. On the Pinjarra reserve we lived in a tin shack with only one room. Mum and Dad had a wooden bed and us kids slept on the floor.

At our camp we grew a few vegies, like strawberries, onions, carrots and potatoes.

One day an old bull came walking through our shack—we only had a bag hanging up for our door. Mum had to chuck us onto the roof to get away from the bull. Another time the bull charged us and we had to hide behind a big old log. We were scared of that bull.

I thought he was dead
Etching 2001

HUNTING WITH DAD

Mum, Dad and us kids moved around a lot. We made our camp where the work was on different properties, but quite often it was in the bush among the trees. We would be woken up early to pack our dinner, then off into the bush to do a day's work.

In the bush we'd see all sorts of wild orchids. Then there was bush tucker to be found. It was during these times that Dad would teach us about bush survival, what to look for and how to find water.

Quite often when we ran out of meat Dad would go hunting. He had a couple of well-trained kangaroo dogs. When he took them hunting the dogs would go a little way in front. When they found a kangaroo they'd kill it, then they'd go find Dad and show him where the kangaroo was. Plenty of times the dogs would get busted up by the roos—they would have big rips on them where the roos had kicked them.

We often went bush with Dad. He showed us animal tracks and taught us to tell by the tracks just how long ago the animals had gone past. He taught us how to make snares for roos. We would find their pad or path going through the fence, and there we'd set a snare.

We often went fishing to Ravenswood, or the Bend, as we called it. We had fishing lines wrapped around old tin cans and used earthworms as bait.

Mum, Renee Nannup (neé Hart) Dad, Peter Nannup and my sister Cecilia

Dad and his nephews would walk for miles along the river spearing mullets. Dad made his own spears. The handle was bamboo, and the barb would be hammered into a shape like a gidgie, which is like a straightened fish hook.

Crabbing was a special time for our family. We'd walk for miles just to catch crabs. After catching a sugarbag full we'd walk back to our camp, which was miles into the bush. Us older girls had plenty of arguments about who should carry the bag full of crabs.

Mum, Dad and us kids were heading back to the dairy farm from Pinjarra one day. We had no food at home, and our transport was a horse and cart. As we went over the railway line I looked over the cart, towards the side of the road, only to see some money with a stick placed over it, as if to keep it from blowing away. I yelled at Dad to stop, then I got out and got the money and gave it to Dad. Then instead of going straight home we went on to Coolup to buy some stores.

Our shack at Pinjarra Reserve

BEANSTICKS AND CHRISTMAS

One Christmas when we were camped out in the bush, Mum and Dad cut beansticks to sell to the market gardeners in Spearwood.

Mum used to say, 'get up really early now, because if you don't you'll be left behind'. We'd have our tucker packed, then off we'd go into the bush for the day cutting beansticks.

That same Christmas Dad bought himself an old Ford ute. The night before Christmas morning, Mum made some jelly and custard. She had a tin of pudding and cream. We had no fridge so Mum put the jelly and custard in the back of the ute to set. So for Christmas breakfast we had jelly, custard pudding, cream, damper, kangaroo and our mugs of tea. We never worried about lunch, although we did have something to chew on, and we always got a Christmas stocking with some goodies in it. We enjoyed what we had.

Old Ford ute
Woodcut 2005

CUTTING FENCE POSTS

As teenagers, when we went home from the mission for holidays and Dad was working cutting fence posts, we would often help him. First he would fell a tree, then saw the tree into the size of posts, one child on each end of the saw. Then Dad would split the logs into posts with several wedges, then we'd pile them up. That sure was hard work.

First he would fell a tree
Etching 2001

PINJARRA RACETRACK

As young children—and there were many of us who lived on the reserve at Pinjarra—very early one morning before any adults were awake, the children would go to the racetrack to see if we could find any money that had been dropped. In those days two shillings was a lot when you had nothing.

This day the children went to see what they could find. My sister and I could see these children getting small bottles of cool drinks and hiding them behind some bushes. We watched for a while, then when they were gone we took their bottles and hid them in our hiding spot.

While we were doing that a car came up to the racetrack. This bloke saw all these black kids and took off back to tell the police. Word must have got around to all our parents that the police would be coming to the reserve, so Mum said to us, 'OK, let's go for a walk to the dump.'

As we were scratching around in the dump the police pulled up. They spoke to Mum then put my sister and me into the police car, took us downtown and put all of the reserve children in jail. There were two cells, the boys in one and the girls in the other. Next minute someone started to cry, then it was on, everybody was crying. We must have stayed there for hours. There was only a single-bed mattress in the cell.

Laurel and cool drink bottles
Woodcut 2005

From there the police marched us all up to our school. I don't know how the state school children got on, but we were marched up to the convent school. The Sister stood on the verandah holding a big cane. As we came in front of her we had to hold out our hands and receive the cuts, and they really stung. A few days later Dad had to go to court about us taking the cool drinks and had to pay for how many bottles we took. But before we went to the dump, Mum must have known the police would check how many bottles we took so she only left out a few bottles.

When I was about seven years old we were camped towards Coolup on a dairy farm and I was still at the convent school. I used to catch the bus into school then out again. One day as I was going down to the corner store to buy my lunch, I saw the school bus parked outside the state school with some children in it. I thought it was taking the kids home. I forgot about my lunch and got onto the bus, but it ended up in Mandurah. I didn't realise that the state school children were only going for swimming lessons. I sat on the bus until they were finished swimming.

Us kids in trouble
Woodcut 2005

WAGGING SCHOOL

When in the convent primary school, we would sometimes wag school. Our parents would send us to school but of course we wouldn't get there. Instead we'd meet under the grapevine at the back of this old empty house, and from there we'd all go swimming in the river. On the other side of the river was an orange orchard. We'd swim over and put oranges in our bathers, swim back and share the oranges out to each other. We always made it home by the time school was out.

Oranges in our bathers
Etching 2001

FIRST HOLY COMMUNION

As a young child living on the reserve at Pinjarra, I made my first Holy Communion when I was about seven years old. Early one morning I got out of bed and walked downtown to the convent, for that was a special day for me. I can still see that day in my mind, all misty and cold.

On arriving at the convent the nuns gave me breakfast and then a bath. Sister then dressed me in a white dress. When all the other children arrived we all went to the church, and afterwards we had a party. I felt like I was an angel that day.

First Communion at Pinjarra
Woodcut 2001

CAMP FIRE

One night we were sitting around a fire with some cousins and sisters and brothers. Our grandfather was telling us some yarns and we were all talking, laughing and just enjoying each other's company. As Grandad was speaking, out of the darkness appeared at least six men. Grandad went over to speak to them, then gave them some food, then they went back into the darkness again. Can't remember if Grandad ever told us who they were.

Grandad's Visitors
Etching 2001

THE LOLLY TREE

This is a story told to me by my cousin. Our uncle, Lionel Hart, one day took his nieces and nephews out bush, for a ride in the cart. When they got to a certain tree, it was just loaded with all these lollies with pretty wrappings on them. They thought it was just wonderful that their uncle should find this lolly tree, and they did not know that he had gone out to the bush earlier to put the lollies on the tree.

Lolly Tree
Woodcut 2001

MISSION DAYS

THE BIG BLACK CAR

One day Mum asked us if we would like to go to Wandering Mission. Being only a small person, I thought this was going to be exciting; we had some cousins there and everything was going to be fine. Mum bathed us in our old tin tub and we had new dresses.

My next memory is of this big black car pulling up and a white lady getting out. Then we were put into the car, sitting there crying for our mum. I don't remember the car leaving our home, I don't remember the trip to the mission. All I can see is all these girls peeping at us. We felt so alone and just wanted to go home to Pinjarra. Everything was so cold. My sister was only six years old and I was eight.

Many times I wondered why Mum let us go. We never got to ask her.

We saw our parents during the Christmas holidays, and if they came to the mission they were allowed to stay for a few days. It was always a relative who would bring them as Mum and Dad did not own a car at that time.

Leaving Home
Woodcut 2001

MY FIRST CHRISTMAS CARD

My first Christmas card was from Mum. It was about Jesus in the manger. It was a nice brown with golden shiny paper on it. When I got my card, well, I had a good cry for my mother.

We never got to open our mail. It was always opened and read before it was handed to us.

We never got to open our mail
Etching 2001

FARM WORK

Years ago, when only girls were at the mission, we used to do farm work like stooking hay, where we had to pick up the bundles of hay and pile them into a heap. You didn't know what would be under the sheaves of hay—could be a snake or a bobtail lizard. And that was scary, 'cause it happened to me. I wouldn't do hay stooking any more after I found a bobtail under the hay.

But once the hay was all put into the big shed, us girls used to wait until we saw the Brothers go in their jeeps, then we used to make for the haystack. We jumped all over that haystack and had such fun, and got all itchy from the hay. Don't know if the Brothers ever found out it was us mucking up the haystack, but it was fun.

There were mornings when we had to have turns getting up when it was still dark to go and milk the cows. I hated that as it was so cold and we had no shoes, just bare feet. One day it was my turn. As I was sitting way back on the stool, leaning forward, just able to touch the cow's udder, Brother Val came along and pushed me just about under the cow. So here I was almost hugging the cow. I hated those smelly cows peeing near me.

After the cows were done, you had to clean out the milking shed and separate the cream from the milk. The cream would later be used to make butter for the staff—us kids got pig or

Stooking hay
Etching 2001

sheep fat on our bread. Then there were the calves to feed, also the chooks and pigs. The little pink piglets were so cute.

We also had a pet kangaroo who used to share the warmth of the fire with us when it was cold. When she grew up she went back to the bush, only to bring her own baby back to us. So they would go back and forth. In this photo you can see her as a little joey.

Our pet kangaroo

SLIDING SISTER

Our dining room was a great big place, and when the children had watermelon to eat some of the seeds would find their way to the floor. It was during one of these evenings, when the kids were feasting on watermelon, that a nun came walking through the dining room. She must have stepped on some of the seeds, because the next thing we knew was Sister sliding along the floor—talk about the sliding nun. The kids got such a shock and everything was silent. Poor Sister, she should not have smiled at the kids, because they just busted themselves laughing —so cruel.

Sliding Sister
Etching 2001

BIRTHDAY PARTY

Many years ago at the mission, when one of the older girls had a birthday, all the other working girls would dress up in ballgowns for the party. First we decorated her place at the table with flowers. Next came the birthday cake with sandwiches and party cakes. Then we would have a dance and play some games. The game I liked was Pass the Parcel, where a large chocolate bar was wrapped up in lots and lots of newspaper, tied with string and more string.

The person who threw the six on the dice had first turn at trying to unwrap the parcel. But before that, you had to put on a hat with gloves and use a knife and fork to start unwrapping the parcel. You'd just get to have a turn at the parcel when someone else would throw a six, then off would come your hat and gloves and your knife and fork would be handed to that person. That game was lots of fun.

Some other games we played were skipping, fly, marbles, rounders, and we had our cubbies too. I used to like making mudcakes, of course out of mud, and decorating them with flowers, then pretending to eat them.

Dressing up for the party
Woodcut 2005

PUMPHREYS BRIDGE

Easter was always a special time of the year. All the kids would go some place, while Sister and some of the working girls would go and hide the Easter eggs. When it was time to find the eggs the kids went wild with joy. Sister often helped the little ones to find their Easter eggs. Everyone had a fun time, because you got to eat so many chocolate eggs. Sometimes on a Sunday all the girls would pile into the mission truck and off we'd go to Pumphreys Bridge for a picnic. Sister would pack our picnic lunch and when we arrived, if the day was fine, there would be lots of swimming in the river. When time came to have our lunch we'd sit under the bough shed. I always loved that place, at Pumphreys Bridge. There were lots of swings and everyone had a really great time.

Us kids on the back of the mission truck at Pumphreys Bridge

FATHER WELLEMS' GARDEN

Old Father had a great big vegetable garden at the mission. There were all sorts of things growing in there, lots of fruit trees. He was always working in his garden. My cousin Avis and I would often go to the garden to get watermelons for the kitchen. We were never told how to tell if the melon was ripe, so we cut triangles into them to see. If they weren't red, we'd turn them over to hide what we did. I don't know if Father ever found out that it was us. The kids had lots of spinach to eat and everyone just hated it. Mulberries were nice when they were out, but the Sisters didn't think too much of them, as we always got our clothes pretty dirty from the mulberry juice. Those were good times at the mission.

Old Father Wellems got so old that he got sent back to Germany where he died.

Watermelon Patch
Woodcut 2001

SPRINGTIME

Spring was such a beautiful time. It just felt so warm and cosy. These were the times that the girls would go bush and come back with armfuls of wildflowers. There was every wildflower you could think of, and they were all so beautiful. I think the Golden Wattle was my favourite; it had such a sweet smell. Then there was the Spider Orchid, which I loved too. At times I do go back to the mission and just walk in the bush.

On warm sunny days when the field was green and covered with clover it was a special place for us girls—many a happy moment we spent laying in the grass thinking of family and friends.

One time the older girls told us that we would grow quickly if we stomped in fresh cow poo. So here we were running about the field looking for fresh cow poo. Can you just imagine how all that muck was squished between our toes?

After the first rains, when all the fields were like a green carpet, all the mission girls would get the washing baskets and go into the paddocks where we would pick hundreds and hundreds of mushrooms. When we got back to the mission Sister would cook up the mushrooms for the girls to have a feed.

Picking berries was also a great time for the girls. We used to fill our pockets with all sorts of berries. Just to go bush was

Us girls in front of the old slide

something special. Down at the creek, the big girls would make swings from the trees and we had many hours swinging from those trees. There was once an old slide in the playground, but the nuns had it taken away because we kept tearing our dresses on it.

Winter time was very cold. The fields used to be all white with frost, and we never had shoes to wear; we only wore sandals to church. But we made big fires to keep warm.

Swings down at the creek
Pencil 2006

GUM-PICKING

Gum-picking would happen on Sundays, when the girls would go for their afternoon walks. We'd walk for miles and miles into the bush. When someone found a gum tree that was loaded with gum, all the girls would come running to see if they could get the most gum off. So if you found a tree you just had to keep quiet and get the gum off quickly before the others spotted you. A lot of the gum was eaten on the spot, and some would be taken back to the mission, where it would be put into a jar with sugar and water. It would get all soft and sweet, then you could eat it with a spoon. But watch out, because after eating that gum there would be lots of smells.

Another special day was when it was Damper Day, or that's what we called it. We took our mixed-up dough into the bush, made a fire and cooked our dampers. This happened at a place in the bush that we called the Springs. There was always water at these big rocks and the girls really enjoyed themselves. Quite often the damper would get overcooked, but there was plenty to share around. When eating was over, the girls just laid around on the big rock in the warm sunshine.

Damper Day at the Springs
Pencil 2006

GIRLS GONE WALKABOUT

Every so often a mob of girls would run away from the mission. They were just trying to get home to their families. Most of the time they never got too far, as the staff would find them and bring them back to the Mission. The girls would often talk about how far they got away from the Mission.

Sometimes the girls would call in to a farm for a drink of water. Then the farmer would ring old Father to let him know they were there. Father would hop into his car and go and pick them up. The girls always got a punishment for running away, like extra work or being grounded. There was this one girl who had no relations; she must have been an orphan. Well, she was with some other girls who ran away, but poor Jessie was the only one to get punished this time. She got a hiding with a strap.

Wandering Mission convent

THAT OLD MISSION BUS

This photo is of the Wandering Mission kids when we came up to Perth, to visit an old friend in Victoria Park. Mr and Mrs Scheurer were like a Father Christmas to us. They would often come to the mission, where they would play games with everyone, and at Christmas they'd bring lots of toys.

Often we'd go up to Perth. Once we went to see the Fire Station. All of us girls on the back of the mission truck—how awful, but that was the only way we got carted around. I still reckon we should have had a bus. In later years the mission did get a bus to take the children out.

Outside the Fire Station on the mission truck

GOODBYE WANDERING

During the Christmas holidays as a seventeen-year-old, I got a job on a dairy farm owned by Mr and Mrs Jackson. The farm was on Stake Hill Road, and every afternoon I would saddle up the horse then ride into the bush calling the cows. With me for company was Mrs Jackson's dog. I forget what his name was but the horse was called Pete and he was all white. Mrs Jackson told me if I ever got lost, just let the reins loose and the horse would bring me home. The cows would know where to go, too. I would help get the cows milked, put the milk into urns for the milk truck to pick up, and clean out the milking shed. Then I'd feed the old bull.

When I left the mission I went out to Karlgarin to help Mrs Hinck do housework. I stayed there for two years. My sister went to Perth to high school and later on to be a nurse, and I went to a lovely family to work and help with the children. They have grown up now and a couple of them have families of their own. I still keep in touch with them.

My family at Karlgarin
Left to right: Nola, Trevor, Laurel, Leanne (baby) and Bernadette

MISSION MATES

This photo is of some of the children at Wandering Mission, on their First Holy Communion Day, which was a very special day for them. A few of the children have now passed on, and a lot of them are now grandmothers and grandfathers.

Sometimes when a new building was to be opened lots of people would come to look over the mission. Everything had to be tidied up and polished, like when we got the new bell for the church. The Bishop blessed the bell. Don't know if it did any good—you see the mission closed down in 1975 and all the children went back to their families.

Nobody lives at Wandering Mission now. They had a caretaker but that's about it. The mission was a cold place; there are so many memories there, some good, some sad. A lot of those children are still friends to each other. These days I still run into some of them, and we often yarn about the mission days and what went on there.

Children at Wandering Mission, on their First Communion Day